Aaron Judge: The Inspiring Story of One of Baseball's Rising All-Stars

An Unauthorized Biography

By: Clayton Geoffreys

Table of Contents

Foreword

Since entering the pros, Aaron Judge has been one of the most impressive hitters of the modern era. Unanimously selected as the American League's Rookie of the Year in 2017, Judge has emerged as a rising star. In fact, in 2017 he won his first Silver Slugger Award which is given to the top offensive player in each position within both leagues. It'll be exciting to track Judge's career over the years as he continues hitting home runs. Thank you for purchasing *Aaron Judge: The Inspiring Story of One of Baseball's Rising All-Stars*. In this unauthorized biography, we will learn Aaron Judge's incredible life story and impact on the game of baseball. Hope you enjoy and if you do, please do not forget to leave a review!

Also, check out my website at claytongeoffreys.com to join my exclusive list where I let you know about my latest books. To thank you for your purchase, you can go to my site to download a free copy of *33 Life*

Lessons: Success Principles, Career Advice & Habits of Successful People. In the book, you'll learn from some of the greatest thought leaders of different industries on what it takes to become successful and how to live a great life.

Cheers,

Clayton Geoffreys

Visit me at www.claytongeoffreys.com

Introduction

Some of the most beloved stories in sports are usually the ones that recount the journeys of those who did not look like they could make it in the big leagues at first but eventually rose to become some of the best athletes in their respective professions and roles. After all, everyone loves a story wherein someone was considered an underdog but continued to work his way up to become one of the best. Underdogs are much more relatable to the general public because many people know what it feels like to be looked at like someone who does not have the talent and the physical capabilities to become one of the greats in their respective fields.

We cheered for the underdog athletes who became some of the best at their craft even though the odds were against them. Jeremy Lin, a Harvard graduate, suddenly became a global sensation in the NBA even though Ivy League players are not known to excel in professional sports. Tom Brady, who was drafted in the sixth round of the NFL, is arguably the greatest quarterback in the history of the sport. You might even consider global football celebrity Odell Beckham Jr. as an underdog since nobody back in 2014 considered him to be the best athlete at his position during the NFL draft, but he quickly rose to prominence to achieve a level of stardom no one had thought possible.

In recent years in the MLB, there seems to be one particular underdog story that has captured all of us because of how unlikely it was for him to become one of the best baseball players in all of America today. And this story really is not difficult to miss because of how literally large the man is. This is the story of Aaron Judge, an underdog in terms of his journey, but certainly not someone you would consider an underdog if you just looked at his size.

Standing 6'7" and well over 280 pounds, Aaron Judge is considered to be the largest player at the outfielder position in terms of body mass in the history of MLB. He has the size that would allow him to hold his own against professional wrestlers, is bigger than LeBron James, and has the powerful body strength that would enable him to stand his ground against offensive linemen in the NFL. But just because he is huge, it does not mean that Aaron Judge was always figuratively one of the biggest players in MLB.

Coming into the league back in 2013 via the MLB Draft, Aaron Judge was not someone who coaches, scouts or experts thought would immediately succeed in the major leagues. He struggled to hit the ball perfectly and was never the most accurate batter at his position, even when compared to subpar batters. His size and strength would have made him a good athlete in other sports, but those physical attributes are not always the most important factors that help an athlete succeed in baseball. Needless to say, he needed a lot of work and was not ready for the major leagues even after getting drafted by the New York Yankees in the first round.

To no one's surprise, Aaron Judge did not even start out his career in the MiLB's Triple-A or Double-A divisions. Instead, the Yankees placed him in a low-level Class A minor league to play for the Charleston RiverDogs after getting drafted. In other words, he had to pay his dues first before the Yankees thought he was even worth promoting to the Class A Advanced league division. They probably did not think he was worth a roster spot in the major leagues, but he sure did work his way up to the Double-A before going to the Triple-A two years after he was drafted in the first round.

Aaron Judge did not last too long in the minor leagues because he certainly did not belong there. The big young man was able to show his talents well while playing for the minor leagues and even got named to both the 2015 All-Star Futures Game and the Triple-A All-Star Game. It was in the middle of 2016 when he got called up to the major leagues as a full member of the New York Yankees roster. But accuracy was his biggest problem during his first year with the Yankees.

Aaron Judge got hurt after spending just a month in the big leagues. At that point, it was as if he had to battle his way through the injury and work his way up for a job the same way he did when he was still in the minor leagues. Judge felt like he was still an underdog even after proving he could make it to the big leagues because he still had to make sure that he could keep his job with the Yankees. Of course, he also realized that other teams were out to get him and would try to take him out of his element by focusing on his weaknesses.[i] Coming into the 2017 season, he thought of himself as an underdog so much so that he did not even try to make himself comfortable in New York—there was still the possibility that he could still get demoted back to the Triple-A.[ii]

Things turned for the better for Aaron Judge, who worked his hardest during the 2017 offseason, right after recovering from his injury. With an entirely new approach to batting, Judge was able to minimize the weaknesses opposing pitchers could exploit while still retaining his amazing power. He demonstrated his ferocious batting power by making ridiculous home runs that were breaking modern-day records. He was also setting records for home runs for a player considered a rookie in the major leagues.

Setting record after record during his rookie year, Aaron Judge quickly became a fan favorite and was winning the attention of the media. He eventually got voted as the American League Rookie of the Year and even finished second for the American League Most Valuable Player Award in just his first full season playing major league ball. Indeed, Aaron Judge belonged in the MLB.

Injuries may have slowed Aaron Judge in his second and third seasons with the New York Yankees, but his star is still on the rise as a former underdog who is now a nationwide sensation. There is still so much for Aaron Judge to do since coming over to the major leagues, but it takes knowing his story to fully grasp how hard he has worked to get to where he is today.

Chapter 1: Childhood and Early Life

Aaron Judge was born on April 26, 1992, in Linden, California, to biological parents he never met or had any contact with. As early as the day he was born, Judge was already an underdog who needed to find another family to take care of him. Luckily for him, a couple was more than willing to give him a fighting chance in life. Adoptive parents Wayne and Patty Judge took baby Aaron in and gave him a home.[iii]

As teachers, Wayne and Patty Judge may not have biological children of their own, but they are more than capable enough to know how to raise children as if they were their own. (Aaron also has an older adopted brother named John.) On top of that, growing up under the parental guidance of the Judges allowed Aaron to not only escape the hardships that would have come had he been left without parents, but it also allowed him to stay grounded in life with parents that knew a thing or two about teaching children.

Thinking back to the day he and his wife adopted Aaron, Wayne Judge thought it was a miracle that they had landed a baby that would not only become a well-grounded young man but who would eventually become a star with the New York Yankees.[iii] But the one thing they already knew back then was that Aaron Judge was going to be a large man. The Judge household often joked that Aaron Judge looked like the Michelin Tire man as a baby because of how big he was, even back then. He was so big that he needed to eat *a lot*—the typical four-ounces of formula per feeding was not nearly enough for him!

Growing up as a child, Aaron Judge had the size that allowed him to excel in sports. Throughout his early life, he was a three-sport athlete who played baseball, football, and basketball. He was bigger than most kids and that made him a really good choice as a center. At the same time, his father also told him the story of Dave Winfield, a baseball Hall of Famer, who was once able to play three different sports because of his size.[iii] Winfield ended up choosing baseball because it was not as physically taxing as both basketball and football. That seemed to be the trajectory of Aaron Judge's life as well during his younger years. He might have played basketball and football, but he loved baseball more.

Aaron Judge spent his early life in Linden, California, which is only about two hours away from San Francisco. As such, Judge grew up a big fan of the San Francisco Giants. He was ten years old when the Giants lost to the Los Angeles Angels back in the 2002 World Series in a seven-game series. He also idolized Giants player Rich Aurilia instead of Barry Bonds, who went on to win five MVP awards during his career in the MLB.[iv]

The reason why Judge loved Aurilia was simple: his dad's favorite number was 35, he played all of his sports wearing 35, and Aurilia wore 35. His love for the number 35 was what led him to enjoy watching

Aurilia, even though he was not a star. Judge often copied Aurilia's stance when he was playing Little League games. To his memory, it seemed funny for him to be doing so because, being a large kid, he had to crouch very low to mimic that stance and looked really awkward as such, but he loved it because of the number 35 and how his father loved to see him wear that number.

Speaking of his number, it was when he was ten years old that he realized there was a possibility that he was adopted. Aaron Judge is a biracial African-American with white and black features. Meanwhile, his parents are both white. This led him to ask questions about why he did not look like his folks. To that end, Wayne and Patty confessed the fact that their son was adopted. But Aaron did not mind knowing the truth because, to him, Wayne and Patty were the only parents he had ever known.

The Judge family raised Aaron to become a humble and very disciplined young man. His parents were both physical education teachers who knew how much being disciplined could help improve a young person's overall mental and physical state. Due to this facet of his upbringing, Aaron Judge carried the same kind of disciplined approach to his game of baseball and was never too eager to hit the throws he was unsure of.

Aaron Judge has always been grateful to his parents for raising him and for teaching him the many lessons he may not have learned had he been raised differently. The family also raised him as a Christian, which has allowed Aaron to stay grounded and thankful for any kind of blessing he received while growing up. To this day, he still believes wholeheartedly that God was the one who matched him with his parents when he was adopted on the day he was born.[iii] He may not have been able to become as good an athlete as he is today had he been adopted by other people. However, both Wayne and Patty believe that they are more blessed to have been given a child with the kind of demeanor and talents that Aaron has.

The humble and very grounded demeanor that Aaron Judge still carries today is also a product of how he was raised in a tight-knit community. Linden is a small town of only about 1,800 people. Growing up in such a small place allowed him to stay true to his roots even though he is now playing in the biggest market in the entire world. The small-town boy stayed in Linden throughout his entire life and even went to Linden High School, where he became one of the school's top athletes.

Chapter 2: High School Career

Aaron Judge stayed home and attended Linden High School even though Linden was just a small farming community. The closest city to Linden is Sacramento, which is not even a major market in sports. Thus, Judge spent his high school years in a small town far away from the typical exposure that most other high school stars get when they are standing out as athletes in their respective schools. In a way, Aaron Judge was still an underdog who was trying to make the most of what he could do as a high school athlete.

Speaking of his years as an athlete, Aaron Judge was a three-sport star who managed to do well in all the sports he played because of his unique blend of size, agility, mobility, and natural giftedness as an athlete. One could say that he was blessed to have a body that was fit to excel in any kind of sport. Aaron Judge was already a prodigy back when he was in high school.

Many star athletes tend to believe that they can focus more on being athletes than being students during their high school years. For them, their sole goal is to one day turn into professional athletes and make much more money than those who focused more on their studies and ended up with good grades and stable jobs. Such is the allure that most high school athletes tended to dream of. The dream of becoming stars in their own sports is what tempts them to turn away from all of the other so-called distractions and just focus on becoming the best in their respective fields. Some would even say that these young men tend to allow their athletic prowess to get over their heads and turn them away from their life as students. That is why the high school athletes who ultimately did not make it big in the pros or even in college very often struggle in life outside of sports. They forgot that school was just as important as their life as athletes. But that was not Aaron Judge.

While Aaron Judge was indeed a prodigious all-around athlete that played multiple sports, he refused to sacrifice his time as a student just to excel in sports. Despite how alluring it really was to become a three-sport athlete that could possibly make it big in any of those three sports he played, Judge did not let sports get in the way of his studies. Instead of choosing to play football alongside baseball and basketball as a high school freshman, he opted to skip that endeavor in favor of focusing more on his academics, since the jump from middle school to high school was not something that seemed so easy for a lot of young athletes to do.[iii] Aaron Judge did indeed play football the following year, however, and he was able to juggle it together with his time as a star in both baseball in basketball. He spent fall playing football, winter starring in basketball, and spring as a standout baseball player.[v] Instead of focusing only on one sport, Aaron Judge played three sports and was really good in all of them. He had a chance to become special in any of those sports thanks to his natural gifts as an athlete.

Aaron Judge believed that playing basketball and football on top of playing baseball helped his overall development as an athlete. It can be argued that high school is the most crucial part of a young athlete's development because that is when he is still growing at his most rapid pace. It is also during high school when athletes start to develop a feel for their bodies and begin to adjust to the new things that they are able to do in an athletic sense. For example, bigger athletes that eventually grow close to seven feet need to be able to develop mobility and coordination during their high school years so that they will not end up as bumbling and uncoordinated giants in their older years. In that sense, a big athlete like Judge would not have developed his mobility and coordination just by playing baseball. Something such as basketball helped him in that regard.

Of course, Aaron Judge himself realized how much playing two other sports helped him with his career as a future baseball star. In basketball, players are required to move constantly out on the court—both on offense and defense. It is a sport unlike any other because everyone out there is tasked to play both ends of the game as opposed to just focusing on either offense or defense. Moreover, basketball is a fast-paced sport that requires a player to move up and down the court countless times in a single game. As such, Judge credits his development as an athlete to his training as a basketball player because it improved his overall conditioning and coordination. It also allowed him to stay fresh and active during the baseball and football offseasons. In his own words, basketball helped him prepare for baseball.[v]

As a basketball player, Aaron Judge played the center position. Even though he is considered by all accounts a huge man, he was actually an undersized center back in high school because he was not as tall as the other centers. But whatever he lacked in height, he more than made up for in heft, strength, and physicality as a large young man. Judge played exceptionally well in his final year as a high school basketball standout and averaged 18.2 points per game.[vi] He was his team's leading scorer and was an All-State selection.

Had Aaron Judge pursued basketball, he might have made a Division I college team as a power forward that could dominate opposing power forwards with his strength and mobility and even stand toe to toe with centers in college. But basketball was not where his heart belonged, although he did admit that this sport helped his overall development as an athlete. And what coaches thought about him as a basketball player was that he seemed a bit too soft and passive. Judge was a nice guy who would rather help an opposing player he had knocked down on the floor rather than help his team score over a disadvantaged defense over at the other end.[vii] To that end, he might not have had the necessary mindset to become a star in basketball. Then there was football.

Aaron Judge did not start playing football until his sophomore year in high school because he wanted to focus more on his academics while he was still adjusting to his new life as a freshman. However, even though his development as a football player was hindered by one year, Judge was still able to show his capabilities out there on the pitch as a standout wide receiver.

To say that Aaron Judge played wide receiver can be somewhat confusing for those who do not know a lot about football. Wide receivers are some of the most important players in football because they are usually the main targets of quarterbacks for catches and are responsible for most of the touchdowns. They need to be able to run as far as possible or as needed by their team's offensive scheme while eluding their defenders to make a catch thrown by a capable quarterback. In that sense, there is a need for a wide receiver to be one of the more capable athletes in football. They should be one of the fastest players on the pitch and probably only second to running backs in terms of overall speed. Wide receivers also need to be well-coordinated and very athletic to be able to move around the field easily and to make tough catches. That is why some of the best wide receivers in the NFL have a good combination of height, speed, explosiveness, and overall athleticism.

In relation to Aaron Judge as a wide receiver, it might come as a surprise that someone as big as he is used to play that position. In the NFL, the average wide receiver's height is somewhere north of 6'1" and is nowhere near the 6'7" that Judge sports.[viii] Miami's Tanner McEvoy, at 6'6", is probably the tallest NFL wide receiver today. While it certainly does help if a wide receiver is big and tall because it allows him to fight over defenses physically and catch passes easier compared to shorter wide receivers, the usual trend is that taller and bigger athletes are less likely to be as quick and mobile as those who are a bit smaller.

A testament to how good of an athlete Aaron Judge was when he was in high school was that he actually excelled as a wide receiver despite his size. He might not have been the fastest player on the pitch, but he was able to use his size and physicality to dominate his defenders and perform like a star wide receiver. His prowess in that position allowed him to set the Linden High School record of 17 touchdowns.[vi]

Turning out to be quite a good football player at his position, Aaron Judge attracted the interest of a lot of college football programs during his later years in high school. It came to the point that schools such as Stanford, Notre Dame, and UCLA started recruiting him to play tight end for them instead of wide receiver because of his size and strength. Because he respected his parents' emphasis on education, there was a reason for Judge to accept those offers from some of the best college football programs. However, his true calling was elsewhere. He always loved baseball more than both basketball and football.

Speaking of the fact that Aaron Judge was a three-sport athlete back in high school, he did admit that he also did not take any of them very seriously. He may have loved playing all three of those sports, but there were always moments wherein he would lose interest, especially when it was near the end of the season for one of those sports. He couldn't wait to play basketball when it was near the end of football season. Likewise, he felt like he needed to play baseball near the end of the basketball season. He never really took those sports as seriously as other athletes did until the time finally came when he realized he could do something special as a baseball player.[vii]

As good of a player as he was in both football and basketball, Aaron Judge chose baseball over those sports not because they were physically easier on his large body but because he felt like baseball was *harder* for him than any of his other sports. He wanted to be challenged by playing baseball. There were more moments when he struggled in baseball than there were in both football and basketball. He enjoyed the negatives of it all, and he wanted to learn from the bad moments he experienced in baseball.[v] He worked hard to improve and focused on every mistake he committed on the field. This allowed him to get better and better every single game, no matter how difficult the grind may have been. This also allowed him to attract the interest of some college scouts even though a lingering football injury let him slip under the radar of some teams, especially considering that he was playing in a small farming town outside of media coverage.

But Aaron Judge was more than just the baseball star who would eventually develop into one of the better players in all of America. He was someone everyone in Linden High School looked up to, literally and figuratively. He was a member of the student government, a good student with a 3.5 GPA, and a model student-athlete who was against the vices that could derail a young person's life. He was always a humble young man who stayed grounded to his roots while making sure he never instigated fights in school or after games. Even students who never cared a bit about sports saw him as a humble young man they could look up to.[ix] Judge was anything but perfect, but he was an ideal student who was capable of carrying that character to any team he chose after his high school years.

Coming into his senior year, Aaron Judge had already committed to the Fresno State Bulldogs as a baseball player. That was when he began to take baseball seriously, even though he was still playing basketball and football. Judge had decided that he was going to make it big in baseball. In that turn, he started dominating the high school ranks as an ace pitcher who could throw the ball so hard that it registered 94 miles an hour on the radar gun.[ix] Fresno State felt lucky they were able to acquire this young man right when his stock as a high school player was not quite high enough for him to attract offers from other notable schools. But he was a different beast in his senior year thanks to his amazing work ethic—that was when he began not only gaining the attention of college scouts but also scouts working for professional teams.

The one surprising thing about some of the scouts' requests was that they were actually asking him to bat after games because opposing teams were not allowing him to swing the bat by throwing him curveballs throughout the game. They were afraid of his power. But the thing about the barrage of curveballs being thrown at him was that it allowed him to learn the value of patience. He had to wait for the right time to swing instead of trying to expand his strike zone. Judge developed the kind of patience needed for a good hitter. He did not have to simply rely on his power all the time, but had to make sure that he was patient enough to know when to hit.[ix]

Other scouts were quick to hear about the big kid playing in the small town of Linden. Those who worked for the Indians and the Yankees heard about what this kid was doing out there on the field. They thought he was raw, but what really struck them was that he was really big and very obviously talented despite his size. To this end, the Oakland Athletics even called him in for a workout. Prior to that, Aaron Judge had never even stepped inside the Oakland Athletics' stadium, even though he was only a few hours away from Oakland. But he was there for the workout and was close to fulfilling his dreams of becoming a professional baseball player even without having played a single college game.

As raw as Aaron Judge was in that workout with the Oakland A's, he was still impressing people who were used to seeing professional baseball players. The Oakland Athletics' scouts kept asking where Aaron Judge was playing in college without even knowing that he was still just a high school senior back then.[vii] It was then and there that the Athletics decided they would draft Aaron Judge if they ever had the chance to do so. Come draft day in 2010, they indeed took him with their 31st-round draft pick, hoping they could help develop him into a star in the future.

Aaron Judge had a chance to go and make money as a professional baseball player while the Oakland A's were waiting for his skills and talent to catch up with his massive physical development, but the young man from Linden decided it was best for him to go to Fresno, where he committed to play before he even made it onto the radars of professional teams. The reason for wanting to go to Fresno was not a selfish choice for him and was not even related to baseball. Instead, he heeded his parents' wishes as they wanted him to get a good education by going to college. As such, he set his eyes on playing college baseball for Fresno State even though he had a chance to go pro right after high school. Of course, it also helped that his parents graduated from the same school.

Chapter 3: College Career

Desiring to fulfill his parents' wish of wanting a good education for him, Aaron Judge went on to attend California State University, Fresno instead of signing with the Oakland Athletics as a player they could possibly hone in the minor leagues in preparation for the major leagues. The good thing about his time with the Fresno State Bulldogs was that he was fully focused on baseball and his studies instead of playing multiple sports. His goal was set—he was going to become a professional baseball player after his collegiate stint.

But Aaron Judge was actually tempted to go to Oakland to become a professional. The Athletics were playing quite close to his home and were offering him a good amount of money. Most young men would go to be a professional for the right amount of money and for a chance to play baseball close to home. However, Judge not only realized that he wanted to go to college to fulfill his parents' wish but also because he thought that he was not yet mature enough to start playing professionally.[vii] He knew that he was physically ready for the pros, but he wanted to develop mentally to take on players older than he was at that time.[x] After all, he was only 18 years old, and he needed to go through a lot of experiences first before he could truly be ready to take on the professionals.

The head coach of the Fresno State Bulldogs, Mike Batesole, was a huge believer in what Aaron Judge could do to the point that he even believed they had got him in a steal after he spent his junior year in high school mostly on the injured list.[vii] It was when Judge stood out during his senior year that everyone on the Bulldogs' coaching staff realized what an unpolished diamond they had waiting to be developed into one of the most precious stones in all of baseball.

Matt Curtis, a coach for the Fresno State Bulldogs, thought that Aaron Judge's main asset was not his power. He may have already been a big man coming into college and was bigger than most other players he was going to be facing in the collegiate ranks, and Curtis saw that Judge did have power, but it was the last thing to come in terms of what he could do out there on the field. Instead, his biggest asset was projection and how far he could go as a player once he not only learned how to hone his power but also his overall skill as a batter.[vii]

Aaron Judge entered Fresno State as an outfielder. This allowed him to make use of the conditioning he developed back when he was still playing basketball and football back in high school. And because of his size, he could make use of the space he was able to take up with just a few steps while also contributing to the powerhouse Fresno Bulldogs team with his overall combination of conditioning and power as a hitter.

Kendall Carter, who works for the Yankees, saw what kind of athlete Aaron Judge already was. He saw how

Judge transformed from a kid who seemed a bit uncoordinated during his senior year in high school to a more mobile giant who could move well around the field during his freshman year in college. Tom McIntosh, who also works for the Yankees, thought that Judge seemingly transformed overnight due to how quick he was to develop during his stint with the Bulldogs. And Keith Snider, a scout for the San Francisco Giants, thought that Aaron Judge was seemingly bigger, stronger, and more muscular during his freshman year in comparison to his senior year in high school.[ix] It was as if he was able to quickly transform just by focusing more on baseball and working hard on it.

It turned out that Aaron Judge's stay with the Fresno State Bulldogs helped him more than he ever thought it would. His body seemingly developed well as it matured to become more muscular and more coordinated than it was when he was in high school. As such, scouts from the professional teams were already projecting how prodigious his power would become once he turned pro. But, at that point in his life, he was still just a freshman—albeit one who had earned a Louisville Slugger Freshman All-American selection. He only hit six home runs during his freshman and sophomore seasons, as it took some time for Aaron Judge to develop.

For Aaron Judge, his time with Fresno State was always about getting a chance to stand up against some of the better players in college at that point because that was one of the ways he could develop into a better player overall. Playing college baseball would allow him to rise up to a level of competition more challenging than what he had experienced when he was in high school. The best part was that he enjoyed playing against the best that college had to offer.[vii]

Aaron Judge showed the full extent of his development in the college ranks when he played for the Brewster Whitecaps of the Cape Cod Baseball League, where a lot of the best college players went to play during the summers when college baseball was in its offseason. Judge wanted to continue to play even during the summer so that there was no halting his development as a future star.

The Cape Cod Baseball League is no joke. It is arguably the best summer baseball league for college students in the entire country and has one of the best rosters of college players. The league has become a steppingstone for former players that are now in the major leagues. In that regard, the Cape Cod Baseball League may be just as difficult or even more challenging than Division I baseball. John Altobelli, the manager of Brewster, said that the Cape Cod League is where college players can prove themselves to be the best. And if they hit somewhere above .250, they would be one of the best hitters in collegiate baseball.[vii] It was a good place for Aaron Judge to try to continue to get better.

Aaron Judge impressed and turned a lot of heads during the Cape Cod Summer League in 2012. What truly made him one of the better performers that year was his size. To that end, scouts from professional teams were so surprised not only by Judge's combination of size and power but were also amazed by how athletic and well-coordinated he was despite being that big.

After playing 32 games throughout that baseball league, Aaron Judge finished with a batting average of .270, which is higher than the .250 average Altobelli was talking about. He also hit five home runs, which is just a home run shy of his total home runs during his freshman and sophomore years. Judge also finished with 16 RBIs and struck out 33 times in those 32 games.[vii] He did not have the best stats during the tournament as other prospects wound up showing better numbers, but Aaron Judge was opening more eyes than any other player because of his combination of size, power, and athleticism.

Aaron Judge may not have ended up with the best stats that summer, but he was one of the main attractions for scouts. Opposing teams and scouts alike had to stop doing what they were doing when Judge was out there batting. His power amazed everyone and the young man from Linden was dropping jaws left and right due to how far he could bat those balls. During games, all of the five home runs he had hit were as impressive as anything scouts had ever seen in the Cape Cod League. With all due respect, he was a monster due to how powerful he was with that bat in his hands.

The Cape Cod League games were played on high school baseball fields, which are much smaller compared to the professional-level stadiums that professional teams play in. Thus, the scouts could not easily gauge how powerful players really were. They could only imagine what they would be like when they got to play in bigger stadiums. However, the Cape Cod League allowed them to do so when all of the teams were set to do workouts in the famous Fenway Park in Boston, Massachusetts.[vii]

Aaron Judge barely remembered what it was like batting in Fenway Park because they only had a limited time to bat and there were plenty of players waiting for their turn. For him, it was kind of rushed, and he did not even remember a lot about the things that happened during what was supposed to be a memorable moment for most college players—batting for the first time in the famed Fenway Park.[vii]

But scouts had a different perspective of what happened during batting practice. There were plenty of players in Fenway Park. All of them were trying their best to put all of their strength into their swings in the hopes of impressing scouts and hitting the ball over the Green Monster, the famous 37-foot high left field in Fenway Park, so that they could have something to brag about after the Cape Cod League. Scouts remembered all of them and how it seemed like it was too much of an effort for them to hit the ball with all that they had. Meanwhile, Aaron Judge was doing it so effortlessly. The young man from Linden swung the bat with such ease and was able to hit the ball with so much power that he was basically doing what other players were doing but with less than half their effort. His power was what struck people the most as the Linden monster was able to hit balls over the Green Monster with relative ease.[vii]

Aaron Judge returned to Fresno State a different man due to the momentum and lessons he gained from playing in the Cape Cod Baseball League over the summer. He improved a lot compared to his sophomore year, but there were still scouts who thought that he was not the best player out there due to how there was something different with his swings.

During batting practices and with scouts out there to watch him hit balls, Aaron Judge was barely hitting home runs because, they thought, of how he was working to improve the mechanics in his swing. Instead, he was hitting line drives that did not look too impressive in terms of their overall verticality, but some scouts were indeed sure that Judge was hitting those balls with so much power that they were probably going at least 115 mph. However, there were still scouts who believed that Judge did not have a lot of power because they only based their assessment on home runs.

Meanwhile, those who truly know how to assess raw talent realized that there was going to be something special in those swings coming from the 6'7" 280-pound hulking young man. There were still those who thought that Aaron Judge had the potential to become a star in the big leagues as a professional. He ended up with a .369 batting average during his junior year in college as a Fresno State Bulldog. His OPS was 1.116 in the 56 games he played that year. He also ended up with a total of 12 home runs to show off his massive power after only hitting six during his freshman and sophomore years. Judge led his team in home runs, RBIs, and doubles. He won a slot to the All-Conference team and was set to end his college career with a bang as Judge decided it was time to move on to the professionals while his stock was still at an all-time high.

Chapter 4: Professional Career

Getting Drafted

As scouts were looking at him when he was showing off his raw and incredible power back in high school, Aaron Judge proved that he had the talent and potential worthy of becoming a first-round pick in the 2013 MLB Draft. Scouts even assessed that he was not going to end up lower than the first round. In that respect, he was able to go further than the 18-year old Aaron Judge, who was taken by the Oakland Athletics as a 31st-round pick in 2010. Judge was going to be a first-round draft pick.

In terms of his physical talent and amazing gifts as a large athlete, there was no arguing the fact that Aaron Judge possessed the size and power of a top-tier player. At 6'7", he had the height of an NBA forward and an NFL offensive lineman. And at 280 pounds, he was bigger and heavier than a guy such as LeBron James and perhaps 95% of the centers in the NBA. He could probably even hold his own against opposing NFL linebackers. And if he wanted to change his career path, he might be big enough to become a force in professional wrestling. All those factors considered, he was set to become one of the bigger, if not the biggest, players in professional baseball. Scouts were even comparing him to basketball star Blake Griffin in terms of his size and what he could do athletically because he simply had no comparisons in baseball, either in the minor or major leagues.[xi]

When you talk about raw power, no scout could deny the fact that Aaron Judge was coming into the draft with the most hitting power out of any prospect. In

44

batting practices, he was an attraction that made scouts and other teams alike stop what they were doing just to watch him swing the bat with so much ease and make the ball travel at ridiculous speeds. While other players were trying so hard just to hit home runs, Aaron Judge did it with seemingly half the effort due to his prodigious combination of size and strength. There was so much power in that muscular 6'7" frame. That said, his signature and most attractive tool in that arsenal of his was undoubtedly his power.

Though Aaron Judge may be big and strong, he is not the bumbling giant that most people are tempted to think just by looking at him. As someone who plays outfield, particularly as a center fielder, he has shown that he is a capable athlete with superb conditioning. Center fielders are generally the fastest of the three outfield positions. What that means is that Judge is someone who has the speed that is expected of someone playing that position even though he is coming into the draft as literally a huge prospect. He is described as a solid runner who may not be the fastest athlete out there on the field, but able to cover enough space as needed because of his size.[xii]

Outside of what he brings from a physical aspect, Aaron Judge has always been described as a patient batter.[xi] Most people who are born with the power that would allow them to excel at the plate tend to try to hit the ball hard every chance they get. In Judge's case, he seems to be really patient at the plate, as he aims to make sure that he gets the best available shot possible instead of just trying to swing at every opportunity. That, coupled with his amazing power, makes him a huge asset for any team to have at the plate.

In terms of his intangibles, scouts raved about Aaron Judge's overall personality because his demeanor and approach to working hard on his game made him someone who would always have the potential to contribute well to any team. He grew up as a humble and well-grounded young man who never showed any signs of being someone who could ruin a team's chemistry. On top of that, he was always a hard worker with the mentality of someone who strives to get better every single day.[vii]

However, there were still problems that plagued Aaron Judge. For one, the most common reason why not many big players excel in baseball is that they are not physiologically inclined to be the best as accurate hitters. Because of his size, Aaron Judge would most likely struggle to hit the ball when pitches are lower in his large strike zone. In that sense, it is always going to be a hit-or-miss situation for someone of his size.[xii]

Another thing to take note of is that position players at Aaron Judge's size and weight do not always succeed in the major leagues. Not many players who are about 6'7" have been able to succeed in the MLB. The only other person close to Judge's size in the MLB was Giancarlo Stanton, who stands 6'6" and about 240 pounds. Other than that, Aaron Judge seemed to be an outlier as far as his size was concerned.

Some scouts also thought that Aaron Judge was not the best type of player to put at the center fielder's position because he was not the fastest player, and his range was limited when he was in college. Many scouts thought he would play better at right field due to his strong arm and his above-average speed. In that sense, there were a lot of reasons to believe that Aaron Judge was a raw player who might have the power to allow him to excel as a batter but has a bit too many downsides presented by his size. He also needed refinement in his game and there was speculation that he only got as far as he had because of his remarkable combination of size, strength, and athletic abilities.

All that considered, there were those who believed that Aaron Judge would be a first-round pick despite not having all the makings of a top pick. Some would even go on to say that he probably was not worth a major league spot and was someone better off developing in the minor leagues for at least a couple of seasons before he would be ready to make a move to the major leagues. As big as he was, he was an underdog in terms of his status because he just did not have a lot of believers and supporters outside of those he had impressed and wowed with his amazing power.

Probably the only person who truly believed that he was worth a shot because of his combined power and athleticism was the area scout for the Cleveland Indians. But the Indians had the number five pick that season and their higher-ups did not believe that Judge was worth the risk of getting taken that high, despite how much their area scout believed in what the Fresno State product could do.[vii] They also did not have another first-round pick and were not in a good position to be able to draft Aaron Judge no matter how much they were willing to take him. The big man was going to be too much of a gamble for them at the fifth spot when there were other players who were more refined and complete from an overall perspective.

The Arizona Diamondbacks were also interested in what Aaron Judge could do just by looking at his raw power. They had numbers 15 and 36 in the draft. But at the 15th spot, Aaron Judge still seemed like a gamble because, as far as the D-backs were concerned, all he had going for him was his power. In fact, nobody thought that Judge was going to get taken before the 20th pick. Meanwhile, Aaron Judge would have probably been taken before Arizona could draft him at 36 because draft picks chosen after 20 seemed to be more unpredictable.

Draft night came, and Aaron Judge was in New York for the first time in his life. Although he was nervous and was unable to sleep due to the anxiety of the draft, he tried to make the most out of his trip to New York and toured the entire city. He even went to Yankee Stadium and looked at the dugout without even knowing that the Yankees were interested in him. As far as he was concerned, the only teams he thought were interested in him were those that played in the west, such as San Diego and Arizona.[vii]

During the draft, picks after 20 were flying, but Aaron Judge's name was yet to be called. Neither the Indians nor the D-Backs took Judge with their early picks and it seemed as though that the teams that were so interested in him were no longer in a good position to draft the Fresno State star. At 26, the New York Yankees had a good shot at Judge, but they chose Eric Jagielo instead. They were picking once again at the 32nd spot and were giving five other teams a chance to draft Judge even though the big young man did not even think that New York was interested in him. It was a gamble on the part of the Yankees.

Luckily for the Yankees, none of the five teams that were picking before their 32nd pick was invested in Aaron Judge. As such, the Yankees were able to grab

Aaron Judge with the 32nd pick overall in the 2013 MLB Draft. Back then, it made sense that Judge was drafted that far in because he did not have the makings of a star but was someone that teams thought was going to have the potential to hit 40 home runs in a year. Aside from that, some teams just did not feel like Aaron Judge was going to be something special in the MLB. But, if teams were to recreate the 2013 Draft, Judge would have surely been one of the top five picks as only he, second overall pick Kris Bryant, and ninth overall pick Austin Meadows developed into All-Stars by 2019. He may have been an underdog when he entered the draft, but he surely towers over everyone else today, both figuratively and literally. The Yankees found a gem in the form of Aaron Judge.

In Judge's case, he truly did not think that the Yankees were going to pick him 32nd overall that year. There were no indications that the Yankees were interested in him. To that end, he even thought that he was going to get chosen a few picks right after the Yankees' 32nd pick and was about to go to the bathroom before his name got called. And while getting chosen by New York was surprising for a man who has lived in a small city throughout the majority of his life, it was a new start for Aaron Judge, as he was about to embark on his journey as a professional player aiming to get to the major leagues.

Minor League Years

About a month after getting drafted, Aaron Judge signed with the New York Yankees and got a $1.8 million signing bonus for it. However, even though he had just signed a contract to play with a professional team, Aaron Judge was humble enough to accept the fact that there was no guarantee he was going to play in the major leagues.[vii] As impressed as they may have been, the Yankees gave no indication that they were going to give Judge an outright roster spot in their major league team. They believed that he still was not ready or even skillful enough to play for the Yankees.

Judge was pure raw power at that point in his career, but he still had his work cut out for him if he wanted to play in the MLB.

Unfortunately for the young Aaron Judge, who was set to start his professional career, he had to miss the entirety of his first year as a professional baseball player. Shortly after signing with the Yankees, Judge tore a quadriceps muscle during a baserunning drill. Due to the severity of the injury, he never got a chance to show what he was capable of that year. Aaron Judge had to miss the entire 2013 season to recover and subsequently rehabilitate his injury.[xiii]

Already an underdog coming into what was supposed to be his rookie year with a slim chance of getting a roster part, Aaron Judge saw another challenge in his career as he was unfortunate enough to get sidelined in the year he was supposed to try to impress the New York Yankees to give him a roster spot, or at least place him in one of their higher-ranked minor league teams.

But, in the middle of rehabbing his injury, Aaron Judge saw a silver lining in what should normally have been a very dark cloud in his career. He was rehabbing his injury in Tampa, Florida, but was able to spend time with baseball stars Derek Jeter and Curtis Granderson, both of whom were rehabbing their own injuries in the same place as Judge. This allowed Aaron Judge to learn a lot from two stars who had already reached the pinnacle of success as MLB stars. He saw how Jeter worked hard to come back from his injury and was inspired by him. Meanwhile, Granderson taught him a lot about what it was to play in the outfield and imparted useful tips to the recovering future star.[xiv]

Learning the value of hard work in the middle of recovering from a serious injury, Aaron Judge was finally able to make his return as a professional player in 2014 when he was assigned by the New York Yankees to the Charleston RiverDogs, a Class A minor league team. Playing the right fielder position, Judge did not show any indication that he was slowed down by his injury as he played 35 games and finished with an impressive .333 batting average, which was good for sixth overall in the league at that time. He also finished third in terms of on-base percentage with .428 while finishing sixth in slugging with a percentage of .530. Judge hit nine home runs during his time in the Class A league. Though he was coming in raw and was still trying to get his bearings after recovering from an injury, Judge was already proving his worth as a player who was more talented than most guys in Class A.

Throughout his stay with the Charleston RiverDogs, Aaron Judge showed that he was not all about power. Other young hitters, with a quarter of the size and strength of Judge, would try to hit every ball the moment they believed they could send it out of the ballpark with a single bat. But, despite having all that strength in those huge arms, Judge was not about to stray far from one of the traits that had allowed him to get to that level—patience.

Aaron Judge himself admitted that, at that point in his career, what he was working on was the mental aspect of his game, even though all the other developing players were trying to work on becoming stronger and faster. But Judge already realized that he needed to work on his mentality and to become more patient throughout what was going to be a grind of a season that required him to play 140 or more games. His patience and mental maturity were beyond his years, as nobody would ever think just by looking at him that Aaron Judge is a man who preaches discipline above all. Well, it also helped that he already had the physical aspects of the game covered. Nevertheless, what was almost an assurance at that juncture was that Judge was well on his way to becoming one of the better young prospects in the minor leagues.

The New York Yankees were keeping a close eye on Aaron Judge's performances and progression. They were impressed by his rapid development and his ability to dominate Class A and quickly promoted him to the Tampa Yankees, their Class A-Advanced minor league affiliate. Judge impressed the Tampa Yankees early, even when he was not playing. His display of raw power during batting practices made the Yankees believe that they could bank on him in the future not only as a member of the High-A team but perhaps maybe as a true Yankee.

Damon Oppenheimer, Yankees' Director and Vice President of Amateur Scouting, said that Aaron Judge was already one of their more valuable players early in the young minor league prospect's career—not only because of his power but also because he was already a complete package as far as his physical tools were concerned. He could run well, make good throws, be graceful, and show a lot of discipline at the plate whenever he was batting. Oppenheimer even pointed out that not a lot of people realized just how talented he was just because he was a huge player.[xv]

Brian Cashman, General Manager of the Yankees, was aware of how quickly Aaron Judge was developing and was always ready to hear some news about his young prospect. Aside from the raw power and athletic capabilities, one thing he liked hearing about Judge was that the young man was a born leader who could gravitate people towards him.[xv] Being able to do awesome things at the plate and on the field was one thing, but leading people was an entirely different type of trait that Judge possessed.

Aaron Judge's hitting coach in Tampa was also just as impressed with his overall personality. He remembered seeing how Judge had struggled in his first game after getting promoted. But instead of feeling sad after his first unsuccessful trip to the plate as a High-A player, Judge actually went back to the dugout with high spirits and started cheering for his teammates. At that moment, the coach knew that Aaron Judge was not only a physical specimen but also a well-raised and well-grounded man who was never all about himself.[xv]

As a member of the Tampa Yankees, Aaron Judge impressed against Class A-Advanced competition. He hit .283 with a .411 OBP, which was good for second overall in the league that season. On top of that, he finished with an SLG of .442 while also hitting eight home runs in the 66 games he played for the High-A Yankees in 2014. Aaron Judge clearly was showing that he was ready for the bigger stage. Aaron Judge undoubtedly impressed the major league higher-ups as he was invited to play as a non-roster player for the New York Yankees during the 2015 Spring Training. He was part of the 26-man lineup who were asked to train together with the main roster, but the Yankees still believed that he had a long way to go before he would be ready for a spot in their major league team.

After a year playing minor league baseball in the Low-A and High-A divisions, Aaron Judge was promoted to the Class AA League to play for the Trenton Thunder for the 2015 season. Judge did not wait to make some noise in his Double-A debut for the Thunder as he immediately showed what he was capable of when he went for three home runs in his first game of 2015. Playing a total of 63 games for the Thunder, Judge finished with batting stats of .284/.350/.510 while tallying a total of 12 home runs as he was still improving his overall game in his second year as a professional player. He was swiftly promoted to the Triple-A Scranton/Wilkes-Barre RailRiders in the middle of the year.

Aaron Judge received some good news in the middle of his second year as a professional when he was selected to take part in the All-Star Futures Game of the MLB held in Cincinnati that year. He was named as one of two Yankees prospects to represent New York in that upcoming game, as Judge was out there impressing everyone in the MLB with his amazing pedigree and sheer dominance in the minor league ranks.

However, despite how impressive Aaron Judge already was at that point in his career, the New York Yankees decided to hold back on bringing him to the major leagues for September call-ups. The Yankees general manager was vocal in saying that he was only willing to call up those he thought were able to help the main team win during the season and was not so interested in how Scranton/Wilkes-Barre was doing. He also said that he did not think that Aaron Judge was good enough to replace their existing starters or key players in the main roster. Moreover, he iterated the fact that Judge was only going to clog up the roster if he was called up.[xvi] In that regard, Cashman was simply vocal in saying that he did not believe Aaron Judge was ready or talented enough to get to the next level even after doing so well in the minor leagues.

The snub from the Yankees only made Aaron Judge work harder than before as he ended the season with batting stats of .224/.308/.373 in the Triple-A league. He had eight home runs in the 61 games he played for Scranton/Wilkes-Barre that season and was showing that he was indeed ready for a shot at the major leagues after that great performance in his Class AAA team.

Aaron Judge was once again invited to Spring Training as a non-roster player for the New York Yankees, but he still started the 2016 season in the Triple-A as a member of the Scranton/Wilkes-Barre RailRiders. Judge was named to the 2016 Triple-A All-Star Game but failed to make it to the festivities due to an injury. He finished the season batting .270/.366/.489 and with an amazing number of 19 home runs in the 93 games he played that season. With those numbers, it was clear that he was not going to stay with the RailRiders much longer that season as the Yankees were beginning to realize that they needed Judge in their roster.

One fateful day, Aaron Judge was eating at a barbeque place with his family and his girlfriend when the manager of his Triple-A team suddenly walked up to him and told him that he was called up by the New York Yankees—not even a day after baseball legend Alex Rodriguez bid farewell to the MLB and the Yankees in his final game of the season.[xvii]

Al Pedrique, the manager, said that Judge needed to move from Rochester straight to the Bronx on that very same day so that he could play his first game of the season as a full member of the New York Yankees roster. His parents drove him all the way to the Bronx in a rental car, all while Judge could not believe that he had finally been called up three years after he was drafted by the Yankees.

The underdog was still an underdog entering his very first season with the New York Yankees. However, Aaron Judge had finally achieved the dream he had been working so hard towards ever since he got drafted.

Two and a half seasons playing minor league baseball had finally paid off and he was on his way to the Yankees to play in the MLB.

Yankees Debut, Injury

Aaron Judge joined the Yankees as a roster replacement for the retiring Alex Rodriguez. And while he might have only been called up by the Yankees to fill a roster spot left by one of baseball's greatest players, Judge was on his way to prove that he was a rising star who had the potential to be one of the greats as well. This was despite the fact that calling him up was not only a product of A-Rod's retirement but also due to the injuries of key players.[xvii]

On August 12, 2016, Aaron Judge finally made his MLB debut as a member of the New York Yankees versus the Tampa Bay Rays. In his first at-bat of the game, Judge immediately impressed everyone by showing off his unbelievable power. He hit a home run to become one of only a bit over a hundred players in

MLB history to hit a home run in their first at-bat. Tyler Austin, the batter before Judge, also hit his first home run. As such, Judge and Austin became the first teammates in league history to hit home runs in their first MLB at-bat.[xviii]

But Aaron Judge was not done. On the second day of the New York Yankees' bout against the Tampa Bay Rays, just a day after making his debut, Judge hit another home run, proving that his first one the day before was not a fluke. Showcasing the strength in that large frame of his, Judge went on to become only the second player in New York Yankees history to hit a home run in each of his first two games in the MLB. The first one to do it was Joe Lefebvre back in 1980.[xix]

Aaron Judge played 27 games during the 2016 season. He finished with a .179 batting average that was far from the usual kind of batting numbers he was accustomed to back in the minor leagues. He also had an OBP of .263 and an SLG of .345. Judge only had two more home runs after the two he had in his first two games. He struck out 42 times during the entire season. He failed to make any more noise throughout the season as he was shelved due to an oblique strain just a month after making his MLB debut with the New York Yankees. Due to the injury, he had to miss the remainder of the season.

Rookie of the Year, MVP Candidate

As good as Aaron Judge was in the minor leagues, he failed to make a splash after his first two games as a member of the New York Yankees. He struck out half the time he was batting and had batting averages that were the lowest he had had since his college days. He truly had power in those arms of his and was able to send the ball past the bleachers. The problem, however, was that pitchers in the major leagues were just too good and were able to find the weakness commonly seen in batters of Aaron Judge's size—the large strike zone.

To that end, Aaron Judge realized that there was probably a large possibility his place in the roster was not going to be permanent, especially when you factor in how his numbers during the 2016 season seemed too subpar for someone who was dominating the minor leagues. He needed to do something to improve his performances and his numbers so that he could at least keep his roster spot with the New York Yankees. He always had power in his large frame, but what he needed to do at that point in his career was learn how to best utilize his power and minimize any weaknesses that pitchers could find in someone of his size and length out there on the field.

Judge determined that he needed to fix his swing and went into the offseason working hard—like the underdog player he was—to make it to the big leagues all over again. He spent a good portion of the rest of 2016 searching for answers on how to become a better hitter. It was also the same problem that former minor league player David Matranga faced when he was trying to improve his hitting numbers back when he was looking for his ticket into The Show as an MLB player. That was when he met a man named Richard Schenck, who helped him become a better hitter even when his career was nearing its end back in 2005.[xx] Matranga, who observed Judge's first month as an MLB player, knew that the young man needed some help.

Enter Richard Schenck, who David Matranga personally recommended to Aaron Judge. Schenck was never someone who excelled at playing baseball, but he had followed the sport his entire life and was able to help coach young athletes to become better batters in his hometown of St. Louis.[xx]

Schenck spent a good portion of his life studying Barry Bonds, one of the greatest of all time and the all-time leader in home runs. He tried to emulate the swinging motion of the great home run king. He realized that he needed to get his barrel up to speed backward toward the catcher even before the bat was going to move forward. What he also did was get his power from the rear leg while planting his lead leg firmly on the ground. He imparted these teachings to his son and to other players who wanted to improve their batting.[xx]

After his own experience working with Schenck, Matranga advised Judge to spend a week learning under the unassuming man. It only took Aaron Judge two days to see the difference in how his swing improved. He already had a fundamentally sound swing, but he learned how to improve it and get it up to par with what would be demanded of him in the MLB, where pitchers are far more accurate than the ones Judge faced in the minor leagues.

Aaron Judge started incorporating the changes in his swing. He was standing a bit farther off the plate than what people were accustomed to. He also toned down that leg kick and started getting more power from his back hips instead of just relying on his large upper body. Judge said that doing so helped him keep his bat in the zone longer while also driving the ball to the right better.

Schenck said that you do not always have to rely on the strength of your upper body and on the exit velocity and the launch angles of your swing. Instead, the first thing that players needed to take note of is the ability to quickly launch and get their bat up to speed. Moreover, by getting the barrel up to speed behind the head, there will be more time for the hitter to see the ball and make the right read and decision. Aside from those two, putting the front foot down was no longer necessary because you only have to rely on the power of the swing to plant the foot while the rear leg gives power to the hips, which snaps the upper body to give it the power it needs for the swing.[xx]

Entering Spring Training, Aaron Judge used Schenck's teachings and improved his batting while also incorporating some of the things his hitting coaches taught him. Alan Cockrell, his hitting coach, emphasized what Schenck said when he told the young big man that there was a need for him to use his lower body more in his swings. To that end, Judge strengthened his back and hips. As A-Rod himself told Judge, he should feel like he was squatting 300 pounds when using those hops for his swings.[xxi]

By using his hips more and making his lower body the center of his swings, Aaron Judge was also able to move his head less often while swinging. A change as small as that can improve a player's performance drastically because he would be able to see the ball better if his head stays firm. It might not improve the power of the swing, but it will help to make hits more accurate since the player will be able to see the ball more and make the right decisions in the middle of the swinging motion.

As impressive as Aaron Judge was when he was improving his swings, what really impressed the coaches was his ability to quickly incorporate what he saw and heard. He was a coachable young man who was never too confident in the tools he had to the point that he did not listen to any criticisms about his form. To that end, whenever coaches told him about certain glitches and fixes he needed to look at, Judge was always ready to make the change and adapt quickly.[xxi] A lot of players may be willing enough to make a change, but they did not have Aaron Judge's natural giftedness at incorporating fundamental changes into his form.

Aaron Judge did not wait to demonstrate what he could do when the season began. He started as the right fielder on Opening Day and had respectable performances compared to last year. He finished with a .250 batting average in his first two games before struggling in the next three. It took until his sixth game for Aaron Judge to finally find his bearings and adjust to the new season as he went on to hit his first home run of the season in a game against the Baltimore

Orioles on April 9th. Then, in the next two games against the Tampa Bay Rays, he had two more home runs. He was finally showing off what all that offseason work was for.

Ever since hitting that home run against the Orioles, Aaron Judge improved his batting average to .308 in the 14 games leading up to their battle against the Baltimore Orioles on April 28th. In that game, Aaron Judge hit two home runs in the same game for the first time in his career and he was instrumental in helping the New York Yankees come back from a 9-1 deficit to win the game. He also finished that game with three RBIs.

What was amazing about that performance against the Orioles on April 28th was the fact that he hit the ball so hard that it set a record for the fastest exit velocity ever measured by Statcast since it had started keeping track in 2015. Aaron Judge set a record exit velocity of 119.4 miles per hour in one of those impressive home runs.[xxii] However, his future teammate Giancarlo Stanton, a man who is known for being one of the strongest hitters in the game, broke that record in 2018 when one of his home runs measured an exit velocity of 121.7 miles per hour.

Proving that he was having the most amazing season a rookie could ever have, Aaron Judge finished the month of April with a total of 10 home runs to tie the rookie record set by José Abreu in 2014 and Trevor Story in 2016. He was aptly named the American League Rookie of the Month because of his performances. On top of that, after starting his first five games with a batting average of about .133, he ended April with batting stats of .303/.411/.750, which are all better than the numbers he had when he was still playing in the minor leagues.

Against the Toronto Blue Jays on May 2nd, Aaron Judge hit multiple home runs in a single game once again after he finished the win with two homers on top of an RBI of four. Against the Blue Jays once again the following day, he hit another home run to lead the New York Yankees to another win. Ever since Aaron Judge's first home run on April 9th, the Yankees had only lost five times.

Although Aaron Judge did not have a month of May that was as impressive as April, his star only continued to rise. He became more and more popular due to his powerful hits and his ability to change the game with his hitting power, marking a meteoric rise as one of the best rookies the game had seen in a very long while. He became so popular that the Yankees put up a three-row section called "The Judge's Chambers", which contained 18 seats for fans who were specifically chosen to wear a courtroom judge's clothes complete with wigs and foam gavels.[xxiii] At that point, there was no arguing the fact that Judge was becoming one of the most popular players in the entire New York Yankees roster—even though he was still just a rookie who, only about a year ago, had been an underdog playing in the minor leagues and someone not many people expected to rise in the majors.

On May 28th, Aaron Judge led the New York Yankees' win over the Oakland Athletics with his first career grand slam, a play where a single home run allows all three bases occupied to score, thereby giving a total of four runs in a single play. The single home run that Judge had in that game gave him four RBIs to seal the deal for the New York Yankees. While he only had seven home runs in May as opposed to the ten he had the month prior, Aaron Judge improved his batting average to .347 to showcase how much more accurate and patient he was as the season progressed. He was once again the AL Rookie of the Month.

After hitting a home run on June 1st, Aaron Judge had a mini drought of home runs. But it was on June 10th when he broke his own personal record, hitting a home run that had an exit velocity of 121.1 miles per hour; Judge broke the record he set two months ago and set a new record for the fastest exit velocity recorded by Statcast. (Again, this would later be broken by Stanton.)

Judge took that momentum with him into the very next game in a win over Baltimore. In that 14-3 win, he went for a perfect 4 out of 4 in his plate appearances and hits while also hitting two home runs in what was arguably his best game as a professional at that point in his career. One of those home runs went an astounding 495 feet due to how hard Judge hit it. That was the longest home run of the entire season. With that hit, Aaron Judge not only had the fastest exit velocity for a home run but also had the longest home run of the season. At that time, there was no arguing the fact that Judge was the MLB's home run king. No other player could hit home runs like he could.

Once again, Aaron Judge was named the AL Rookie of the Month and even went on to lead the AL in all three Triple Crown categories thanks to his amazing performances at that point in the season. He was even voted in as an All-Star for the 2017 MLB All-Star Game after leading the entire American League in votes garnered. Needless to say, Aaron Judge had achieved superstar status in both play and fame just a year after he was just some minor league player who thought of himself as an underdog with no assurances of ever getting to the major leagues.

On July 7th, Aaron Judge reached legendary rookie status when he recorded his 30th home run of the season. With that, he broke a record previously held by Joe DiMaggio to become the leader for most home runs hit by a Yankee rookie. He also became only the second rookie in league history to hit 30 home runs just before the All-Star break to prove that he still had a lot of home runs left in him when the season continued after the midseason break. And during the All-Star break, he won the Home Run Derby in spectacular fashion to lay claim to the crown as the

MLB's undisputed king of home runs. He became the first rookie to ever do so outright.

Aaron Judge did not let the All-Star break stop his momentum. On July 21st, in a win against the Seattle Mariners, he went on to have a total of four home runs in a single game. Judge hit the ball in one of those home runs so hard that it seemed to have bordered the impossible. The exit velocity of that home run was so fast that Statcast could not even record it.[xxiv] One could only speculate how fast the ball traveled and how far it went. And while Giancarlo Stanton holds the record for the fastest exit velocity ever *recorded* by Statcast, we can only assume that the home run hit by Judge on July 21, 2017, is the true record in the Statcast era of the MLB.

As the season progressed, Aaron Judge eventually slowed down due to the wear and tear of playing in his first full MLB season. During the month of August, he was able to hit a total of only three home runs. He also had a pretty bad month of August, with batting averages of .185/.353/.326, which were below his normal stats. Nevertheless, that did not stop him from doing spectacular things. On August 16th, he hit a home run that traveled a distance of 457 feet.

Aaron Judge piled up record after record during the early portion of September. On September 4th, he hit the 100 mark for walks to become only the first American League rookie to have at least a hundred walks in a single season since Al Rosen did it back in 1950. He also became only the first player in the entire MLB to do so since Jim Gilliam did it as a rookie back in 1953. Then, six days later in a win over the Texas Rangers, Judge recorded his 107th walk, which is the most walks a rookie has ever had in a single season since Ted Williams did it way back in 1939. Also, on September 10th, he became only the second rookie in MLB history to have at least 40 home runs in a season since 1987. He, Babe Ruth, Lou Gehrig, Joe DiMaggio, and Mickey Mantle are the only rookies to hit 40 or more home runs in a single season before turning 26.^{xxv} And what was most impressive about that accomplishment is that you have to go all the way back to 1956 for the last time a rookie aged 25 or younger was able to hit 40 home runs in a season.

Aaron Judge continued to hit the ball hard day by day as the season was nearing its end. On September 25th, he hit two home runs in a win over the Kansas City Royals to reach the 50 mark for home runs in a single season. By doing so, he surpassed Mark McGwire's rookie record of 49 home runs in a single season. Judge's stats that season were not only great for a rookie but were also bordering Babe Ruth territory.

Against Toronto in the Yankees' final game of the season, Aaron Judge hit a home run to reach a total of 52. By doing so, he was able to break Babe Ruth's single-season New York Yankees record for most home runs. He did so right in Yankees stadium and in front of the New York faithful.[xxvi] Nobody thought a

Yankee would ever break the Babe's record but Judge did so in his rookie season as he was quickly becoming one of the best players the franchise has ever seen in its long and storied history. And while Aaron Judge still had a long way to go before he could truly become as great as Babe Ruth, the fact that he was able to break a long-standing record proved that he was one of the few players who could reach Ruth's greatness and perhaps become the face of the entire MLB.

The season ended with Aaron Judge averaging batting numbers of .284/.422/.627. He had a total of 52 home runs and 114 RBIs on top of a league-leading 128 runs. It was no surprise that Aaron Judge was unanimously chosen as the American League Rookie of the Year. Highly impressive for a rookie, Judge also received a lot of votes for the AL MVP Award but ended up in second place to the 2017 American League Most Valuable Player, José Altuve.

Nevertheless, Judge helped lead the Yankees to a 91-71 record to earn the team a Wild Card spot in the American League playoffs. They defeated the Minnesota Twins in the Wild Card game, wherein Aaron Judge had his first career postseason home run. In the next round, the Yankees defeated the top-seeded Cleveland Indians in five games; Judge had a total of three home runs in that series against the Indians. However, after a hard-fought seven-game series against the eventual World Series champions, the Houston Astros, the Yankees bowed out of the postseason in the League Championship Series.

Aaron Judge may have failed to get his team to the World Series and win a title for them, but he still ended up with what is now arguably the best season a rookie could ever have in the history of the MLB. This was just a year after he was called up by the Yankees when Alex Rodriguez decided to retire from the game and when Judge seemingly had no clue as to whether or not he was going to make it to the MLB someday.

This also happened just a year after Judge's first month in the MLB ended prematurely due to an injury and without any assurance of whether he was going to keep his roster spot.

However, Aaron Judge is now the face of the franchise after putting up the best rookie season anyone might ever have in the MLB. He restored the New York Yankees' place in the MLB and was a game away from reaching the World Series to complete what would have been a Cinderella rookie run for the large man who was seemingly an underdog just two years ago. The sky was the limit for Judge and he was about to use his amazing rookie year as his springboard for success.

Second Season, the Largest Center Field in League History, Injury Year

After what was a historic rookie season that saw him break record after record—stats that had stood for decades and had once seemed unbreakable—Aaron

Judge was on his way to become the New York Yankees' key player heading into his second season as a professional MLB player. Playing for a team as popular and as historic as the Yankees, Judge was carrying the hopes of a franchise heading into the future.

However, Aaron Judge's momentum had to be cut temporarily. In November of 2017, he had to undergo surgery to fix and clean up a left shoulder injury that had started bothering him back in April. He played his entire rookie year with that injury but was still able to put up historical stats and nearly led the Yankees to the World Series in just his first year with the team.

Aaron Judge spent the offseason resting and rehabbing the injured shoulder in preparation for what was going to be another grind of a season coming in 2018. Judge's mindset did not change even after putting up great numbers in his first full season with the team. He still regarded himself as an underdog and he was not going to take anything for granted. For him, he was still trying to win a job on that roster even though he had already proven himself as one of the best players in the entire MLB in just his first year with the team.[xxvii]

Entering Spring Training of 2018, Judge did not think about holding back even after recovering from his injury. He did not even think his injury was an excuse for him to not work any harder than he did when he was still trying to win a roster spot on the Yankees as a minor league player. Such is the mindset needed of any team from their best player. In the Yankees' case, they needed Aaron Judge to think of himself as an underdog given the fact that the team was entering the 2018 season as the favorites in the American League and as one of the favored teams to actually win the World Series.[xxvii]

Speaking of the Yankees, the team was coming into the 2018 season as one of the more talented squads in the entire league. Back in December of 2017, they acquired one of the most talented hitters in the entire league when they traded for Giancarlo Stanton, the 2017 National League MVP and the only other player in the entire MLB to hit 50 home runs during the 2017 season. That meant that the Yankees were coming into the 2018 season with the two strongest hitters in the entire league and fans could not help but feel excited for the team.

Aaron Judge, who played the right field during his rookie year, moved to the center field because of Giancarlo Stanton's presence. Stanton, the proven MVP, was better off at the right field spot. As such, there was a need to put Judge in center. This made Aaron Judge the largest center field in MLB history in terms of his height and body mass at 6'7" and 280 pounds.[xxviii] Walt Bond, who also stood 6'7", used to be the largest player to play the position, but Judge outweighs him in terms of overall body mass.

It took six games into the 2018 season for Aaron Judge to hit his first home run in his second full year in the MLB. It was in a win versus the Tampa Bay Rays on April 4th. Judge ended the first month of the season with averages of .317/.453/.584 while hitting seven home runs. He was on pace to have a season that was similar to his rookie year. Judge was showing no signs of slowing down from the left shoulder injury he had suffered a year ago.

Aaron Judge had a better month of May with eight home runs. However, his overall averages saw a slight dip as he finished with a BA of .263, an OBP of .386, and an SLG of .579 in the 25 games he played that month. On the good side of things, the Yankees only lost eight games that month thanks to the talented squad that they had even though Judge was not quite playing up to par. Judge's numbers dipped again in June after he went for .234/.321/.489 in 25 games. But again, the Yankees only lost eight games that month.

Even though Aaron Judge did not have a season that was as spectacular as the one he had a year ago, he was still one of the more stellar performers in the league and went on to get selected as a starting outfielder in the 2018 All-Star Game. At that point, he had 25 home runs, 58 RBIs, and a batting average of .277, which were close to the numbers he had a year ago.

Misfortune would strike Aaron Judge once more in July. On July 26th, against the Kansas City Royals, his right wrist was hit by a fastball traveling 93 miles per hour. That forced him to leave the game and it was later revealed that he had fractured a bone in his right wrist and had to recover from it. The good news, however, was that no surgery was needed to correct his injury and he only needed time to let it heal. Initially, it was reported that Judge would require three weeks for his recovery.

The Yankees preferred to err on the side of caution in Aaron Judge's case. It took longer than the initial three-week timetable for him to recover from his injury, as Judge was out for almost two months to rest that fractured right wrist. And though he was out for two months, his team preferred it that way to make sure that he recovered at a steady and controlled pace rather than to rush things. Judge made his return on September 14th against Toronto. He struggled to get back to form after returning from his injury and finished his final 13 games with a batting average of .220 and only one home run.

During the 2018 season, Aaron Judge finished with batting averages of .278/.392/.528, 27 home runs, and 67 RBIs. His numbers that season were down compared to his rookie year, as injuries had slowed him down and limited him to only 112 games during the season. However, even though he might have had a down year, Aaron Judge finished 12th in the AL MVP voting and was still one of the better hitters in the entire league. He finished second to Giancarlo Stanton for most home runs in the team, but he would surely have finished with at least 40 home runs had he been healthy. The Yankees still managed to win 100 games even after missing Judge for nearly two months.

Aaron Judge and the New York Yankees made the postseason by winning the Wild Card game against the Oakland Athletics. Judge had a great game against the A's by going for a home run and a batting average of .667, but the Yankees eventually fell to the Boston Red Sox in a four-game series that saw them only winning one game to bow out of the postseason earlier than most people had expected for a team with so much talent.

Even though Judge did not have a very productive season after coming back from his injury in the middle of September, the postseason was different. He had spectacular individual performances throughout the entire postseason as he went on to finish those five games with three home runs and batting stats of .421/.500/.947. Unfortunately, he was only one man as the Yankees were outclassed by the Red Sox in the AL Division Series by the eventual World Series champions.

Third Fastest to 100 Home Runs, Wilson Defensive Player of the Year

Banking on what was a very impressive 2018 postseason performance, Aaron Judge proved that his right wrist was no longer bothering him as he was heading into the 2019 season with a lot to prove—not as an individual player but as a winner on a very talented team. He had already shown his greatness as the MLB's home run king. Now, it was up to him to show that he could win when it mattered most.

In just his first 20 games of the regular season, Aaron Judge was as impressive as any other player could be when he went for five home runs, 11 RBIs, and a batting average of .288. He was once again on pace to have a really good season, not only as a master of home runs but also as an accurate hitter. But, once again, he was unfortunately sidelined due to a left oblique strain that took him out for two months.

Aaron Judge made his return on June 21, 2019, after a lengthy recovery. He immediately went back to work and went on to have a .333 batting average in the seven games he played in June. He also had two home runs to help give his team a 6-1 record in the first seven games he played since returning from his injury.

Although Aaron Judge missed getting named an All-Star because of all the time he had lost due to his injury, he still had a milestone season that year. On August 27th he hit his 17th home run of the season against the Seattle Mariners to reach the 100 mark for career home runs. Needing 371 games to reach that mark, Aaron Judge became the third-fastest player in league history to reach 100 career home runs. Ryan Howard, who needed 325 games to reach 100 home runs, sits at the top. Meanwhile, Judge's teammate Gary Sanchez reached the mark earlier that season in his 355th game to become the second-fastest player to get 100 home runs.[xxix] Slowed down by injuries in the past couple of years, Aaron Judge would surely have been able to reach the 100 mark faster had he been healthy.

The season progressed and Judge continued to pile up home runs and terrific performances to help his team head into the postseason on a strong note. Playing on a powerhouse team with a lot of strong and accurate hitters, Aaron Judge helped the 2019 New York Yankees become the franchise leaders for home runs in a single season by hitting his first home run over the Green Monster on September 8th when they visited the Boston Red Sox at Fenway Park.

By the end of the year, Aaron Judge finished with 27 home runs and 55 RBIs. He had batting averages of .272/.381/.540 in the 102 games he played that season. Judge helped the New York Yankees finish first in the AL with a record of 103-59. However, as great a batter as he is, Judge proved that he was not just an offensive force that season.

Many regard Aaron Judge as a lumbering giant whose only role on his team is to hit balls as hard as he can to give his team some runs. After all, nobody would ever expect someone as big as him to be a two-way force on the field since most players with that kind of size are merely there for what they can do on the offensive end. However, that was not the case for Judge that season.

Aaron Judged had a total of 19 defensive saves for a right fielder that season to tie for the most of any player at his position that year. What was even more impressive was the fact that he had missed a total of 60 games but still managed to stay on top. He was named the Wilson Defensive Player of the Year at the right field position due to his amazing efforts as a deceptively quick, mobile, and well-coordinated athlete on the defensive end.[xxx]

Leading his team into the postseason, Aaron Judge helped beat the Minnesota Twins in the Divisional Series to get to the American League Championship Series for the second time in a span of only three seasons. However, he struggled against the Houston Astros in a similar way as he did two years ago when the two teams met each other in the League Championship Series. In what was a six-game loss to the Astros, Judge finished with a batting average of .240 and only had a single home run in what was a poor postseason performance for him, and the New York Yankees once again bowed out of the postseason a series short of making it to the World Series.

Chapter 5: Personal Life

Aaron Judge was adopted by Wayne and Patty Judge on the day that he was born. He is of white and black descent and looked nothing like his parents, which is why, at ten years old, he already suspected that he might have been adopted. Both Wayne and Patty were physical education teachers who taught Aaron the value of discipline and education. Since he grew up in a Christian family, Judge is also a devout Christian and has always been active about sharing his faith online in his social media accounts.

One of Aaron Judge's ways to motivate himself is by keeping a note on the Notes app on his phone. The note says ".179," which was the batting statistic he had when he was just called up by the Yankees back in August of 2016. The reason why he uses that as motivation is to make sure that he will never be as bad a hitter as he was when he had just come up from the minor leagues to join the Yankees.[xxxi] He has since batted more than .270 every year since his rookie year.

While Aaron Judge may be a very motivated star who has already reached All-Star status in the major leagues, he still maintains the same humble personality that got him to the dance in the first place. His high school friends and his coaches back in Linden all rave about how he still manages to stay as humble as he always was when he was still growing up in his hometown.[xxxii] He gets so humble at times that his friends often forget that they are talking to a baseball superstar.

Aaron Judge has a girlfriend named Samantha Bracksieck. They made their relationship official on the social media platform Instagram back in 2019. She was often seen supporting Judge and the Yankees during the postseason together with her friend Chase Carter, who was rumored to have been linked with Aaron's Yankee teammate Giancarlo Stanton.[xxxiii]

Chapter 6: Legacy and Future

Aaron Judge may have started his career in the MLB in 2016 after getting drafted back in 2013 and spending time in the minor leagues, however, he has already carved out his own legacy, following in the footsteps of the former greats that have donned the

New York Yankees uniform in the long history of one of the most storied sports franchises in the entire world.

Judge, being a Yankee, has some large shoes to fill as he is now arguably the face of the franchise and should very well live up to the standards set by former Yankee players and legends such as the all-time great Babe Ruth, Derek Jeter, Lou Gehrig, Joe DiMaggio, Mickey Mantle, and Mariano Rivera among others. However, because he plays the outfielder position, he is carrying the torch once held by legends such as Ruth and DiMaggio.

As early as his rookie season, Aaron Judge was already literally and figuratively big enough to fill the shoes left by the greats that have come before him. As legendary as Babe Ruth is, Judge came out of the gate swinging and broke the all-time great's franchise record for most home runs in a single season. Of course, Aaron Judge did it in Yankee Stadium, just a block away from the house that Ruth built. With 52 home runs in a single season, he became the franchise leader in home runs in a year. And during that same season, he also broke DiMaggio's record for most home runs hit by a rookie in a single season. In that regard, he seemingly reached Ruth and DiMaggio territory in just his first year in the league.

Although Aaron Judge's numbers dipped in the next two seasons due to injuries, it can only be speculated that he may eventually reach the career numbers set by both Ruth and DiMaggio if he stays healthy throughout his career and if he manages to last in the MLB as a Yankee for more than a decade. After all, he is the MLB's home run king.

Speaking of his status as a home run king, Aaron Judge did not get that accolade just by being big. At 6'7" and 280 pounds, he might have the size and power to send balls flying through the stadium at any given time. However, his size also comes with a definite weakness that the best pitchers can exploit as he has a larger strike zone compared to smaller hitters. What that means is that someone as big as he is will find it more difficult to hit balls with definite accuracy.

However, by working hard on fixing his form and by focusing on patience and discipline as a hitter, Aaron Judge has learned to minimize the weaknesses that come with his size and improved greatly as an accurate hitter to the point that he actually finished second in MVP voting in the American League during his rookie season. His hard work paid off as his improved form and dedication to look for the best available shot at the ball allowed him to become quite the accurate hitter.

That said, Aaron Judge starts his own personal legacy as a former underdog who worked hard on his craft without having to rely solely on his size. A lot of players with his strength can get away with hitting the ball with so much power, but Judge wanted to be great. Instead, he not only worked on his power but also honed his accuracy to become a more complete hitter that could send the ball flying at a league-high average of about 96 miles per hour any time he wants. He even hit the ball so hard at one point that Statcast could not record its exit velocity.

While Judge is yet to win a championship and a major individual accolade, there is no arguing the fact that a healthy Aaron could very well go down in league history as one of the greatest to ever play the game. He has already proven his all-time great power as a hitter and has broken records because of it. All he needs to prove now is that he is a winner who could very well end up as a World Series champion if his health cooperates and if his teammates do their part as well.

Final Word/About the Author

I was born and raised in Norwalk, Connecticut. Growing up, I could often be found spending many nights watching basketball, soccer, and football matches with my father in the family living room. I love sports and everything that sports can embody. I believe that sports are one of most genuine forms of competition, heart, and determination. I write my works to learn more about influential athletes in the hopes that from my writing, you the reader can walk away inspired to put in an equal if not greater amount of hard work and perseverance to pursue your goals. If you enjoyed *Aaron Judge: The Inspiring Story of One of Baseball's Rising All-Stars,* please leave a review! Also, you can read more of my works on *Serena Williams, Rafael Nadal, Roger Federer, Novak Djokovic, Richard Sherman, Andrew Luck, Rob Gronkowski, Brett Favre, Calvin Johnson, Drew Brees, J.J. Watt, Colin Kaepernick, Aaron Rodgers, Peyton Manning, Tom Brady, Russell Wilson, Gregg*

Popovich, Pat Riley, John Wooden, Steve Kerr, Brad Stevens, Red Auerbach, Doc Rivers, Erik Spoelstra, Michael Jordan, LeBron James, Kyrie Irving, Klay Thompson, Stephen Curry, Kevin Durant, Russell Westbrook, Anthony Davis, Chris Paul, Blake Griffin, Kobe Bryant, Joakim Noah, Scottie Pippen, Carmelo Anthony, Kevin Love, Grant Hill, Tracy McGrady, Vince Carter, Patrick Ewing, Karl Malone, Tony Parker, Allen Iverson, Hakeem Olajuwon, Reggie Miller, Michael Carter-Williams, John Wall, James Harden, Tim Duncan, Steve Nash, Draymond Green, Kawhi Leonard, Dwyane Wade, Ray Allen, Pau Gasol, Dirk Nowitzki, Jimmy Butler, Paul Pierce, Manu Ginobili, Pete Maravich, Larry Bird, Kyle Lowry, Jason Kidd, David Robinson, LaMarcus Aldridge, Derrick Rose, Paul George, Kevin Garnett, Chris Paul, Marc Gasol, Yao Ming, Al Horford, Amar'e Stoudemire, DeMar DeRozan, Isaiah Thomas, Kemba Walker, Chris Bosh, Andre Drummond, JJ Redick, DeMarcus Cousins, Wilt Chamberlain, Bradley Beal,

Rudy Gobert, Aaron Gordon, Kristaps Porzingis, Nikola Vucevic, Andre Iguodala, Devin Booker, John Stockton, Jeremy Lin, Chris Paul, Pascal Siakam, Jayson Tatum, Gordon Hayward, Nikola Jokic, Bill Russell, Victor Oladipo, Luka Doncic, Ben Simmons, Shaquille O'Neal, Joel Embiid, Donovan Mitchell, Damian Lillard and Giannis Antetokounmpo in the Kindle Store. If you love basketball, check out my website at claytongeoffreys.com to join my exclusive list where I let you know about my latest books and give you lots of goodies.

Like what you read? Please leave a review!

I write because I love sharing the stories of influential athletes like Aaron Judge with fantastic readers like you. My readers inspire me to write more so please do not hesitate to let me know what you thought by leaving a review! If you love books on life, basketball, or productivity, check out my website at claytongeoffreys.com to join my exclusive list where I let you know about my latest books. Aside from being the first to hear about my latest releases, you can also download a free copy of *33 Life Lessons: Success Principles, Career Advice & Habits of Successful People*. See you there!

Clayton

References

[i] Mazzeo, Mike. "Why Yankees' Aaron Judge considers himself an underdog entering spring training". *New York Daily News*. 13 February 2017. Web.

[ii] Apstein, Stephanie. "All Rise". *Sports Illustrated Vault*. 15 May 2017. Web.

[iii] Kernan, Kevin. "'Blessed' Yankees prospect elicits Stargell, Stanton comps". *New York Post*. 11 March 2015. Web.

[iv] Miller, Randy. "Why Yankees' Aaron Judge mimicked his childhood hero, Giants' Rich Aurilia". *Newjersey.com*. 16 July 2017. Web.

[v] Amore, Dom. "Here comes the Yankees' Judge: he's the real deal". *Hartford Courant*. 10 July 2017. Web.

[vi] Apstein, Stephanie. "Powerful Yankees slugger Aaron Judge stands out, but all he wants to do is blend in". *Sports Illustrated*. 9 May 2017. Web.

[vii] Feinsand, Mark. "Here's how the Yankees landed Judge in the '13 draft". *MLB.com*. 29 May 2018. Web.

[viii] Stuart, Chase. "Average height of defensive backs and wide receivers". *Football Perspective*. 13 May 2019. Web.

[ix] Braziller, Zach. "Where Aaron Judge comes from explains who he is". *New York Post*. 6 May 2017. Web.

[x] Ballew, Bill. "SAL notes: Yanks' Judge advocates patience". *MLB.com*. 15 May 2014. Web.

[xi] Brady, James. "2013 MLB Draft scouting report round-up: OF Aaron Judge". *SB Nation*. 3 June 2013. Web.

[xii] Wells, Adam. "Aaron Judge: Prospect Profile for New York Yankees' 1st-Round Pick". *Bleacher Report*. 7 June 2013. Web.

[xiii] Ballew, Bill. "SAL notes: Yanks' Judge advocates patience". *MiLB.com*. 15 May 2014. Web.

[xiv] Santasiere, Alfred. "Feature on prospect Aaron Judge – in the Spring issue of Yankees Magazine". *MLB Blogs*. 23 February 2016. Web.

[xv] Feinsand, Mark. "Yankees prospect Aaron Judge has a huge future in pinstripes". *New York Daily News*. 7 March 2015. Web.

[xvi] DiPietro, Lou. "Yankees' September call-ups will be 'all hands on deck' - except Aaron Judge". *YES*. 28 August 2015. Web.

[xvii] Samuel, Ebenezer. "After A-Rod's final game, Yankees call up Aaron Judge and bat him 8th vs. Rays". *New York Daily News*. 13 August 2016. Web.

[xviii] Suss, Nick. "Yanks duo 1st to HR back to back in 1st AB". *MLB.com*. 13 August 2016. Web.

[xix] Kussoy, Howie. "Yankees' Aaron Judge shows off power with encore

Day 2 homer". *New York Post*. 14 August 2016. Web.

xx Mazzeo, Mike. "How Richard Schenck turned Yankees slugger Aaron Judge into the most feared hitter in the American League". *New York Daily News*. 9 March 2018. Web

xxi Witz, Billy. "How Aaron Judge built baseball's mightiest swing". *The New York Times*. 17 July 2017. Web.

xxii Davidoff, Ken. "The Aaron Judge craze hits stunning peak after stunning shot". *New York Post*. 29 April 2017. Web.

xxiii Snyder, Matt. "LOOK: Yankee Stadium now has 'The Judge's Chambers' in right-field seats". *CBS Sports*. 22 May 2017. Web.

xxiv Tsuji, Alysha. "Aaron Judge apparently broke Statcast with an insane home run that nearly left Safeco Field". *For the Win*. 22 July 2017. Web.

xxv "Aaron Judge hits 40th, 41st home runs, as Yankees crush Rangers". *The Denver Post*. 10 September 2017. Web.

xxvi Nathan, Alec. "Aaron Judge Breaks Babe Ruth's Yankees Record for Most HRs at Home in a Season". *Bleacher Report*. 1 October 2017. Web.

xxvii Kelly, James. "New York Yankees: Aaron Judge approaching spring training with fire". *Elite Sports NYI*. 20 February 2018. Web.

xxviii Hascup, Jimmy. "MLB history: Yankees' Aaron Judge ties for tallest center fielder to ever play". *USA Today*. 31 March 2018. Web.

xxix Goldberg, Rob. "Video: Yankees' Aaron Judge Becomes 3rd-Fastest Player Ever to Hit 100 HRs". *Bleacher Report*. 28 August 2019. Web.

xxx Stepien, Garrett. "Yankees' Aaron Judge among MLB's 2019 Defensive Player of the Year Awards". *SNY*. 6 November 2019. Web.

xxxi "From .179 to the All-Star Game: The climb of Aaron Judge". *USA Today*. 10 July 2017. Web.

xxxii Red, Christian. "Aaron Judge's high school coaches say he was always a humble star". *Daily News*. 16 June 2017. Web.

xxxiii Hendricks, Jaclyn. "Aaron Judge, girlfriend Samantha Bracksieck are still going strong". *New York Post*. 28 November 2019. Web.

Made in the USA
Las Vegas, NV
09 November 2020